JAN 1 5 2011

WITHDRAWN FROM LIBRARY

Exploring the Ancient World

ANCIENT EGYPT

Jane Shuter

Gareth Stevens Publishing

Please visit our Web site, www.garethstevens.com. For a free color catalog of all our high-quality books, call toll free 1-800-542-2595 or fax 1-877-542-2596.

Library of Congress Cataloging-in-Publication Data

Shuter, Jane.
Ancient Egypt / Jane Shuter.
    p. cm. — (Exploring the ancient world)
Includes index.
ISBN 978-1-4339-4158-0 (library binding)
1. Egypt—Civilization—To 332 B.C.—Juvenile literature. I. Title.
DT61.S642 2011
932—dc22
                                2010014425

This edition first published in 2011 by
Gareth Stevens Publishing
111 East 14th Street, Suite 349
New York, NY 10003

Copyright © 2011 Wayland/Gareth Stevens Publishing

Editorial Director: Kerri O'Donnell
Art Director: Haley Harasymiw

Photo Credits:
Ronald Sheridan, Ancient Art and Architecture Collection Ltd, 9, 10, 11, 14–15 (M. Jelliffe), 19, 20–21, 21 (top left), 30, 32, 33, 36, 39, 44–45 (top), 52 (top), 54, 55, 59; AKG Photo Library 7, 22 (Erich Lessing), 25 (Erich Lessing), 42–43 (Erich Lessing), 56–57 (Erich Lessing); Axiom Photographic Library, James Morris 5, 17, 27, 40, 41, 60; C. M. Dixon 6, 12, 18, 26, 31, 37, 38, 48, 49, 51, 57, 58; E. T. Archive 29, 34–35 (Louvre, Paris); Shutterstock *cover* and 1; Werner Forman Archive 8 (Egyptian Museum, Berlin), 24 (British Museum, London), 28 (Schimmell Collecton, New York), 44 (British Museum, London) 46 (University College, Petrie), 47 (Metropolitan Museum of Art, New York), 50 (Egyptian Museum, Cairo), 53. (Metropolitan Museum of Art, New York), 50 (Egyptian Museum, Cairo), 53.

All rights reserved. No part of this book may be reproduced in any form without permission from the publisher, except by reviewer.

Printed in China
CPSIA compliance information: Batch #WAS10GS: For further information contact Gareth Stevens, New York, New York at 1-800-542-2595.

Contents

Egypt and the Nile	4
Before the Pharaohs	8
Ancient Egypt	12
Egyptian Society	14
Religion and Ritual	28
Art and Architecture	38
Everyday Life	44
Egypt in Decline	54
The Legacy of Egypt	58
Timeline	61
Glossary	62
Further Reading and Web Sites	63
Index	64

Egypt and the Nile

Where Is Egypt?

The map below shows where Egypt is. It also shows the two things that most affected how the ancient Egyptian civilization worked—the Nile River and the desert all around it. The river and the desert affected where people chose to live. They also isolated Egypt. The river has several cataracts along it—places where the river becomes impassable rapids. It was therefore not easy for ancient Egyptians to have contact with other civilizations. Because Egypt was hard to reach, it was more difficult to conquer. This may be one reason why ancient Egypt flourished for so long.

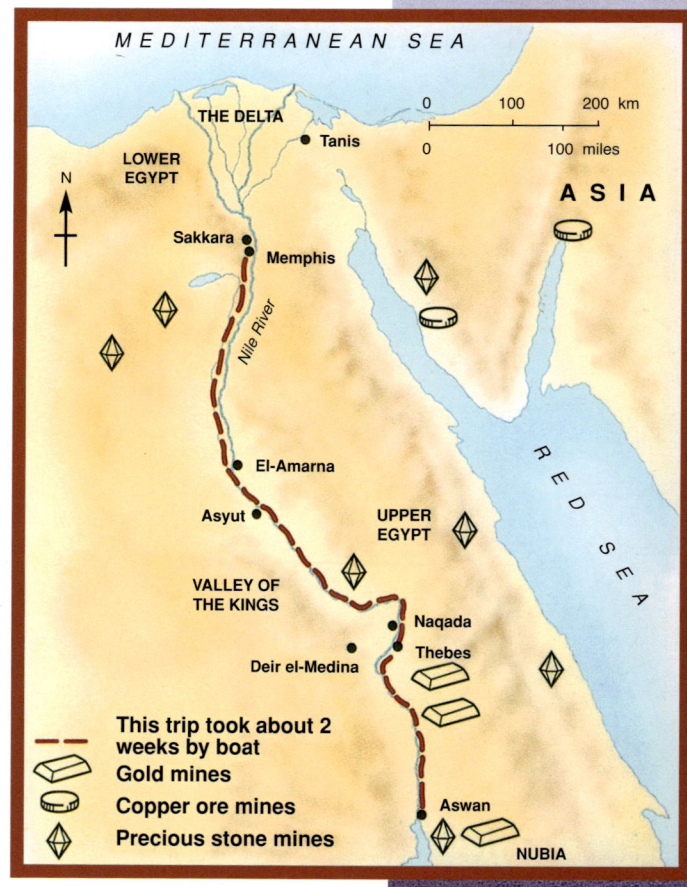

▶ This map shows where ancient Egypt is. It also shows places mentioned in this book.

▶ Life in Egypt today is still shaped by the river and the desert.

Ancient Egypt flourished a long time ago. Egyptians were building and decorating elaborate tombs and temples while the people of Europe still lived in huts. The first Mexican step pyramids were built about a thousand years after those of Egypt.

The first Egyptians had settled along the Nile River by 4000 BCE. By about 2600 BCE, people were living in groups all along the riverbank and working together to provide the things they needed. This period lasted for about 1,500 years—a very long time for any early civilization to continue. From the seventh century BCE, other countries invaded Egypt and settled there. Ancient Egypt became part of the empires of other countries and lost its separate identity. The time line on page 61 shows this in more detail.

River and Desert

The Egyptians saw their land as divided into two parts, the red land and the black land. The red was the desert; the black was the fertile land along the banks of the Nile.

People lived along the banks of the Nile, where the land was made fertile by yearly flooding. This was also the only place that crops could grow. So the Egyptians built settlements strung out along the river with their farmland all around.

▼ **The river was the main form of transportation in Egypt. There were very few land vehicles, apart from chariots. This picture is a painted relief of a hippopotamus hunt in a papyrus swamp, from the Old Kingdom.**

The river had a great effect on the way people worked. It flooded every year. This flood time was called the inundation. The year was divided into three parts. The first part, the inundation, lasted from July to October; at this time all the farming land was underwater. Many farmers did other jobs during this period. From November to February, the land was plowed and the crops sown. From May to June was harvest time. During the period of plowing and harvesting, many people left the other jobs they had to go and work on the land.

The division between the fertile black land and the scrubby red desert was very obvious. It did not run straight as a ruler along the banks of the Nile. But the point where one became the other was always clear. A person could stand with one foot on fertile land and the other foot on desert sand.

The desert kept the Egyptians in and other people out. The Egyptians traded (and fought) with other countries, but, cocooned by the desert, they were mostly self-contained. The Egyptians used the desert to bury their dead. But it was also useful for the living.

◀ The Egyptians were among the first people to mine metals and semi-precious stones on a large scale. Some of their mines ran deep underground. This map—possibly the world's oldest map—shows the layout of one of the gold mines and Basanite caves of Wadi Hammamat, near the Red Sea coast.

It was full of resources. The stone blocks for building the pyramids came from the desert. So did copper, gold, and semiprecious stones. Although most mines were worked by professional miners, the gold mines were worked by prisoners who had been sent there as a punishment.

Mining was difficult and dangerous. So was transporting things to and from the mines. Most of this was done by boat. An ancient Egyptian story tells of a shipwrecked man who met one of the gods: "The serpent god asked what I was doing on his island. I said I was going to the mines, for my lord the King of Egypt. And my boat was big and strongly built; a hundred feet long and thirty feet wide. I had one hundred and twenty sailors, the best in Egypt. But when we got into the open sea, a storm blew up. The ship broke up. All the sailors were drowned. Only I survived."

Before the Pharaohs

When the earth originally was formed, Egypt was underwater. The water level slowly lowered and the land emerged. Egypt began as fertile grasslands, with all sorts of animal life. Over thousands of years it dried out, leaving the Nile River's yearly flooding as the only source of fertile soil.

The first Egyptian people we know about were nomads who moved around hunting, fishing, and mining flints about 700,000 BCE. The nomads did not usually settle: one of the earliest settlements was a hunting and fishing camp at Edfu about 25,000 BCE. By 12,000 BCE people were growing some crops, mostly barley. By 6000 BCE, groups of settlers were farming on a bigger scale, growing food and raising animals. They were also making pots and baskets. As time passed the settlers developed more skills. They began to produce many different objects: pots, mats, cloth, baskets, copper tools, and bone combs.

▼ *This pot, decorated with giraffes, comes from Nagada in Upper Egypt. It shows that by about 3500 BCE, settlers were not only farming but also developing other skills, like making pottery. They also had time to spare and the skill to make their pottery beautiful, not just useful.*

We know of two main and separate areas of settlement. The first was in Lower Egypt, around the Delta and the Fayoum. The second was in Upper Egypt, near Asyut. The people of Upper Egypt may have developed more quickly than those in Lower Egypt. Both groups farmed in the same ways. But, from about 4500 BCE, the people of Upper Egypt made things that were more skillfully decorated. They decorated their bodies, too. Thin, flat pieces of stone were used to grind makeup. They had also begun to make jewelry, mostly simple strings of beads.

About 3500 BCE, the people of Lower Egypt began to build mud-brick houses. They started to use picture writing, too. They made pots on potters' wheels, instead of by hand from coils of clay. They made better tools. This spurt of development may have been set off by trading contact with other countries, but there is not enough evidence to be sure. We do know that soon after this, about 3100 BCE, Lower and Upper Egypt were united by King Narmer, the ruler of Upper Egypt. Everyone now began to live in the same way. This was the start of the Early Dynastic Period.

▲ **This is a small board for the "serpent" game, a game where you race to reach the center of the board (the "eye" of the coiled serpent). The game was played with stone marbles and lion-shaped pieces or counters.**

Most of what we know about ancient Egypt comes from archaeological excavations. Archaeologists have not found many early Egyptian sites, so our ideas about the early Egyptians come from studying a small amount of evidence. Because Egypt used to be more fertile, there could be many more early Egyptian settlement sites in what is now desert. Also, since people still live along the riverbanks, there could be a lot of evidence under modern settlements and fields.

Once Upper and Lower Egypt were united, the new rulers had a large area to govern. The settlements they controlled were strung out along the river. It took over three weeks to sail from one end of the kingdom to the other. So if the rulers were to keep control, they had to find a way of organizing such a huge kingdom.

It was at this time that the city of Memphis began to grow. The rulers of Egypt ran things from there. Because it was at the meeting point of the two kingdoms of Upper and Lower Egypt, Memphis was a good place to choose as a capital. It was also about halfway along the length of the new kingdom of Egypt, which made sending messages easier.

Writing developed quickly at this time. Memphis was well placed for sending messages all over the kingdom, but writing was necessary to communicate these messages. It would also have been much harder to rule the kingdom without being able to record instructions and to keep count of food, animals, and people.

◀ *This man, called "Ginger" by archaeologists because of the color of his hair, died about 3200 BCE. Ginger was buried in the hot sand of the desert, which preserved his body by slowly drying it out and soaking up the fluid to stop the body from rotting. Ginger was buried with food and personal belongings. The early Egyptians probably believed he would need these things in the afterlife.*

◀ *This garnet and gold diadem was made about 3200 BCE. It shows that the Egyptians were mining gold and semiprecious stones at this time. It also shows that some of their jewelry makers were very skilled.*

Between 3100 BCE and 2649 BCE, other skills developed and became important in Egypt. Pottery and jewelry became more complicated and highly decorated. Making these things became a craft that had to be learned. So, although people worked on the land in busy times, they also worked at a variety of specialist skills.

Egyptian religion was also developing. The way people were buried shows that the Egyptians believed the dead came back to their bodies; so they needed the bodies, food and drink, and belongings from their past life to have with them in the next life. Besides making mud-brick buildings, the Egyptians began to build special buildings out of great blocks of stone, so the buildings would last longer. The first of these are thought to have been temples and pyramids.

Although we talk about "towns" and "cities" in ancient Egypt, they were not towns and cities as we know them today. Because there was so little fertile land, there was no real separation between the town and the country, as there was in some other countries where more fertile land was available. All settlements in ancient Egypt had houses, workshops, and land around them that was farmed. Some of the settlements were bigger than others, but everyone was involved in farming at the busy times of the year, and even in the "cities," it was just a short walk to where crops were grown.

Ancient Egypt

Ancient Egypt

The civilization we usually call "ancient Egypt" lasted over 1,500 years, from 2649 BCE to 332 BCE. There were four periods of rule by strong rulers: the Old Kingdom (2649–2150 BCE), the Middle Kingdom (2134–1783 BCE), the New Kingdom (1550–1070 BCE), and the Late Period (661–333 BCE). These were broken up by Intermediate Periods, when governors of areas of Egypt tried to take over the lands they were supposed to run for the kings of Egypt. The one major period of change in ancient Egypt was from 1353 BCE to 1335 BCE, when Akhenaten the ruler of Egypt reorganized the Egyptian religion. Even though the change came from the ruler of Egypt, it did not last long after his death.

▼ *This is the side view of the coffin of a doctor. It includes texts to help the doctor find his way around the afterlife. One thing that did not change much in ancient Egyptian times was the belief that the spirit of the dead went to the underworld after death and returned to the body later. The Egyptians preserved bodies. They also left food, drinks, and transportation for the dead person.*

The Intermediate Periods, times of disruption, gave not only Egyptian governors the chance to seize power from weak kings, but also foreigners a chance to invade. One Egyptian writer's description of the Second Intermediate Period shows why the Egyptians preferred to have strong rulers:

"For what cause I know not, invaders from the East marched into our land, confident of victory. They easily seized it without striking a blow, burned our cities, and pulled down our temples to the ground. They treated the people badly, killing some and selling others into slavery."

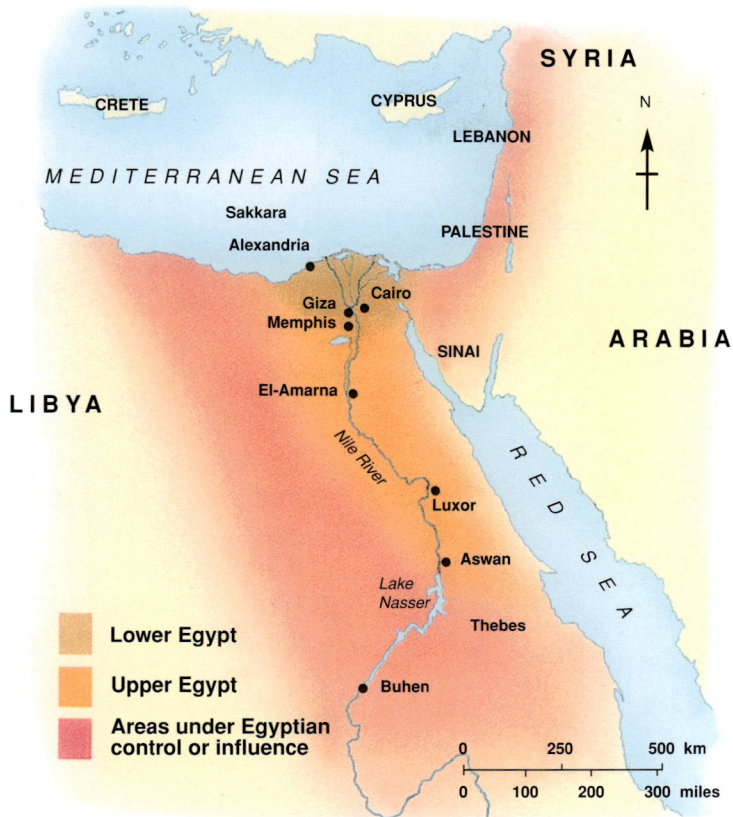

▲ A map showing ancient Egypt at its largest. The Egyptians were not really interested in building an empire. They just wanted to extend their lands along the Nile River and keep anyone else from taking them. Lake Nasser did not exist at the time; it is a reservoir created behind the huge dam that was built at Aswan in the 1960s. The dam was designed partly to keep the level of the Nile more or less constant throughout the year and to prevent it from bursting its banks.

Akhenaten was an unusual ruler. He tried to change the religion from the worship of many gods to the worship of just one god, Aten. He also said that people should draw things differently. This was not a small change, because people had been painting in the same way for hundreds of years, and paintings were an important part of daily life. Akhenaten also built a new capital city, El-Amarna, on the edge of the desert. He ruled there with his queen, Nefertiti, who was also perhaps the daughter of Akhenaten's successor, Ay. Nefertiti had a lot of power at El-Amarna. After Akhenaten's death things quickly went back to normal.

Egyptian Society

How was ancient Egypt run? The gods were at the top level of Egyptian civilization. The slaves, at the bottom, were the least important. Everyone, even the gods, fitted into a particular place in society. They could not change that place easily. Children were expected to follow in their parents' footsteps and to do the same work at the same level. People were taught to be proud of their work.

Ancient Egyptians made a careful distinction between what men and women could do, even among the gods. Women were not seen as less important than men, but they were seen as different. There was work that women were not allowed to do, and work that men were not allowed to do. One of the very few female pharaohs, Hatshepsut, spent her entire rule behaving as if she were a man. During her reign she built a lavish temple in her own honor. Twenty years later, Thutmose claimed the throne and tried to destroy most of her great memorial.

Most people in ancient Egypt had more than one job. They had to work for the pharaoh for a certain number of days each year. This duty work, or unpaid labor, had to be done. Some people had one main job, such as potter or weaver. Scribes could have several jobs; most of them were priests as well as government officials. That was because both jobs were considered to be working for the pharaoh, who was seen as a god as well as a ruler.

▼ *This relief comes from Sakkara. It was made about 2500 BCE. It shows cattle being taken for inspection; owning cattle was a sign of being an important person in ancient Egypt.*

Scribes worked as priests and government officials, but they had the same level of responsibility in both jobs. So someone who was a high priest would also be an important official running a city, or even a whole area, for the pharaoh. Horemkenesi, who died about 1000 BCE, was an ordinary priest. He was also chief scribe at Deir-el-Medina, keeping the accounts of the village that had been built specially for builders working on the royal tombs.

Egyptian Officials

There were officials to organize every aspect of life in ancient Egypt, such as the duty days when everyone had to work for the pharaoh. Usually this was work in the fields or on building projects. Ancient Egypt had canals, dams, and huge temples and tombs. All these things had to be designed by engineers and architects, and many different kinds of craftsmen worked on them. But the work of hauling stones and digging ditches was done mostly by people working on their duty days. There were very few slaves in Egypt.

Officials also organized the collection and handing out of food. They organized beer brewing and winemaking. They ran royal workshops, which made everything for the palace—from mats to jewelry. They ran the markets, setting prices and weights of goods being bought and sold. As early as 2500 BCE, there was a police force. By 1320 BCE there were river police, too.

The ancient Egyptians were good engineers, considering that the only tools they had were made of soft copper or flint or other hard stones, and their only equipment was rollers and possibly wooden levers. Some of their more complicated projects would not have been possible without a lot of organization. Mines were also being dug out all through this period; they were worked using just oil lamps and light reflected from the surface by bronze mirrors.

Pharaohs

The kings of ancient Egypt were called pharaohs. They were said to be children of the gods and chosen by the gods to rule. The pharaoh was the most important person in ancient Egypt. He ruled the country. He was also the most important priest, so he was head of the religion of the country as well. A strong ruler, like Akhenaten, could change the way the country and its religion were run. But a weak ruler could be turned into just a figurehead. The power in the country was then taken over by the most powerful and important government official, the Grand Vizier. Sometimes, under weak pharaohs, the governors of areas of the country could try to take over complete control of their regions.

> In ancient Egypt, people wrote books about how to behave. Most of this advice had to do with the responsibilities of your position, in relation to people who were more important or less important than you. In both cases, people were advised to be good listeners:
> "Teach your son to be a hearer, one who will be valued by the nobles.
> One who guides his speech by what he has heard, one regarded as a hearer."

The word *pharaoh* means "the great house" or "palace." It was used to talk about the rulers of Egypt because it was considered rude to refer directly to someone who was partly a god. So the people talked about "the palace" instead, and everyone knew who was being referred to. By the New Kingdom, "pharaoh" had became a title, like "king." Although people still believed that the pharaoh got his power from the gods, they no longer believed that he was a god himself.

The pharaohs lived in huge palace complexes, such as those at Memphis and Thebes. Palaces had everything a pharaoh and his family might need: kitchens, workshops, temples, and leafy gardens.

Pharaohs were buried in imposing tombs, too. They were buried in pyramids, then in huge tombs cut deep into the rock in the desert, difficult to find from outside.

The reason for making the tombs so big, and so hard to get into, was simple; pharaohs had to be buried with everything necessary to live as grandly when they came back to life as when they were alive. So their tombs were full of treasures. Pharaohs knew that this might tempt robbers. It certainly did, because the only royal tomb to be found intact was that of Tutankhamun, the young king who ruled shortly after Akhenaten. We know very little about Tutankhamun's rule, yet he is one of the most famous pharaohs. That is because the treasures of his tomb survived, and they tell us a lot about him.

Women could be queens, but it was almost unthinkable that a woman could be pharaoh. The most famous female pharaoh, Hatshepsut, ruled by behaving as if she were a man. She used the titles of male kings and dressed in male royal clothes. She ruled only because the next male in line was a boy, too young to take over.

▶ **Pharaohs used four symbols to show they ruled Upper and Lower Egypt. The vulture goddess of Upper Egypt and the cobra goddess of Lower Egypt are shown on this headdress belonging to Tutankhamun. The flail he holds is another symbol of Upper Egypt; the crook symbolizes Lower Egypt.**

Scribes

The pharaoh ruled Egypt, but the scribes ran it. Scribes were the people who were trained to read and write the complicated Egyptian language. Only about 1 percent of the population could read and write. Anyone who was part of the government had to be trained as a scribe. Boys, usually the sons of scribes, were trained at special schools. These schools were in royal palaces, at temples, or in the homes of local scribes, depending on the importance of each boy's family. They learned the writing used in Egypt for ordinary letter writing and accounts. They also learned hieroglyphics, which were used on more formal documents and in tombs and sculptures. They studied mathematics, including how to divide up a yearly amount of grain or beer among workers so that each had the same daily ration.

▼ *Scribes worked sitting cross-legged. Hardly anyone in ancient Egypt could read or write, so there would be a scribe in every town or village whom people could pay to write out letters or documents.*

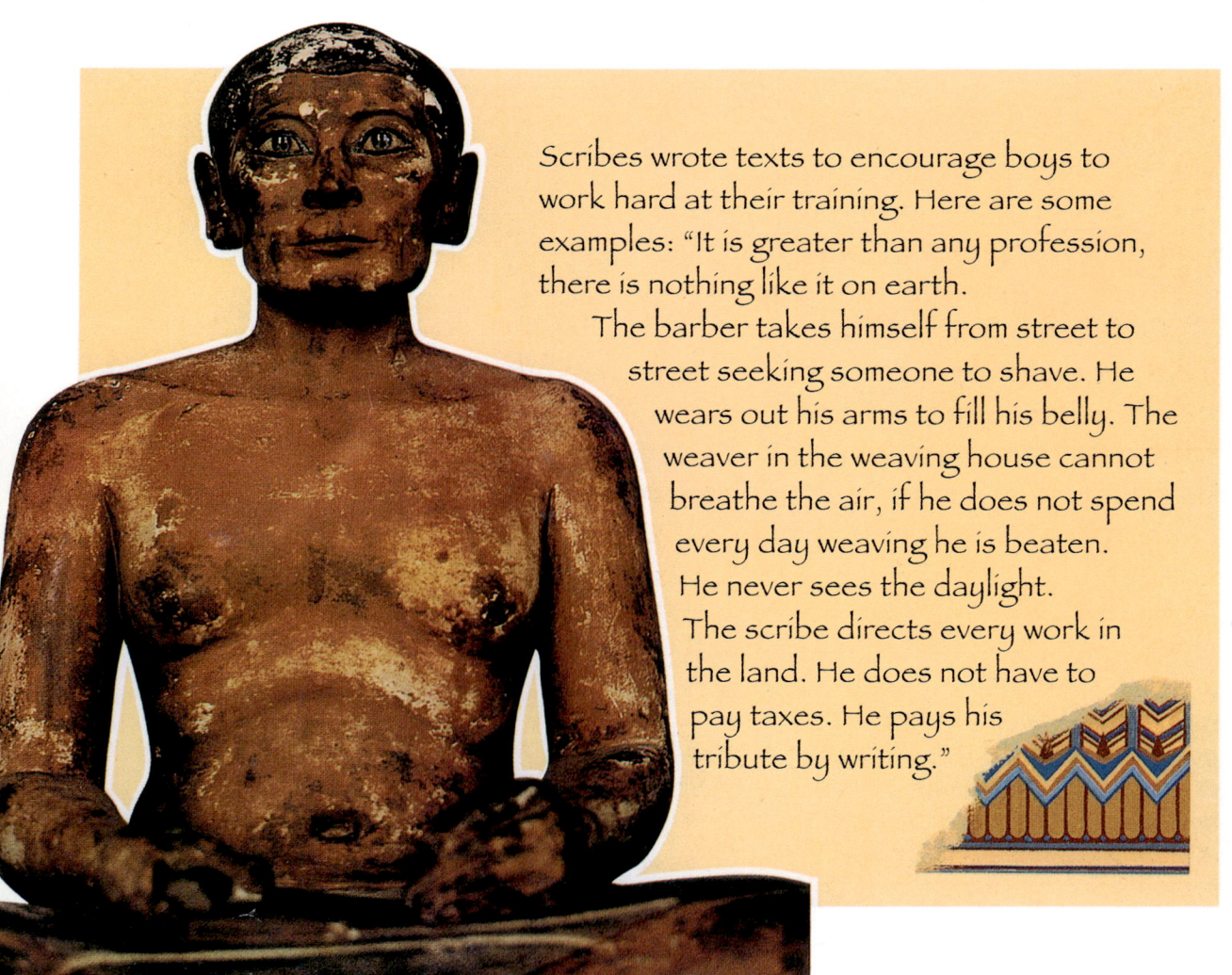

Scribes wrote texts to encourage boys to work hard at their training. Here are some examples: "It is greater than any profession, there is nothing like it on earth.
 The barber takes himself from street to street seeking someone to shave. He wears out his arms to fill his belly. The weaver in the weaving house cannot breathe the air, if he does not spend every day weaving he is beaten. He never sees the daylight.
 The scribe directs every work in the land. He does not have to pay taxes. He pays his tribute by writing."

◄ This palette dates from about 1400 BCE. Scribes wrote mainly in red and black ink, using reed brushes or pens. They wrote on a sort of paper made of papyrus reeds or on leather or wooden boards covered with a white plaster layer that could be wiped clean like a slate.

Training to be a scribe was hard work. But after their training, scribes had privileged lives. Scribes were the only people who did not have to do duty work on the land or building sites. Instead, they made the lists of people who did.

Some scribes were more important than others. Some were made governors of parts of the country; others worked for the government at a lower level: they were sent to check and record the stones that marked the boundaries of farmers' lands when the floodwaters went down; they checked the amount of grain in the royal granaries; and they kept the records at a royal tomb-building site. Some scribes worked on the estates of rich men, keeping count of their animals and grain stocks. Most Egyptian paintings that show people working have a scribe tucked away somewhere, busily recording everything that is going on. Scribes could have more than one government job. They also worked as priests in nearby temples, because priests had to be trained as scribes anyway.

Craftsmen

Egyptian craftsmen used their skills to make items that other people wanted. Potters made dishes, cooking pots, and containers of all shapes and sizes. Weavers made rolls of linen cloth. Carpenters made furniture and smaller decorative things, such as wooden combs and makeup containers. Leather workers made sandals. Stone workers made containers of all shapes and sizes out of polished stone. Jewelers and metalworkers often worked together, to make necklaces, bracelets, vases, and boxes out of precious metals and stones.

▶ **This jeweled collar shows the vulture Goddess Nekhbet. It comes from the tomb of Tutankhamun, from about 1330 BCE. Nekhbet was the goddess of Upper Egypt.**

▼ **Jewelers at work, from the tomb painting of Sobekhotep, from about 1400 BCE.**

The embalmers who made mummies were seen as craftsmen, too. Craftsmen learned their trade by working with their fathers; boys were expected to follow their father's trade. It was hard to change jobs and find work doing something else.

Some craftsmen ran small businesses from a room in their homes. Other craftsmen ran bigger businesses. They employed several workers and had separate workshops rather than working from home. This allowed them to manufacture more, so they could increase their profits. Craftsmen sold things directly from their workshops.

Craftsmen also sold things from stands in the markets that were held regularly in towns. We are not sure if Egyptian craftsmen traded with other countries. This may have been done by the government alone. The Egyptians did not use money to trade. They swapped things or used metal pieces of a set weight (called *deben*) as money. Some craftsmen worked in the royal workshops or on a rich man's estate, rather than working for themselves. They did not make as much profit, but they had regular payment instead. They also had a real chance to stretch their skills. They would be given the materials to work with and, because they were working for rich men, could make things that would have been much too expensive to sell to ordinary people.

Because of the way the Egyptians viewed craftsmanship, the dividing line between those who were regarded as craftsmen and those who were seen as ordinary workers is hard to understand today. For example, a man who washed the clothes at the river might argue that he was a craftsman because he had a skill that anyone else, say a jeweler, was not allowed to take over from him. Some of the writings of the time seem to make a clear distinction between people such as potters and jewelers on one hand and people like barbers, fishermen, and laundrymen on the other.

Working on the Land

Farming was a very important job in ancient Egypt. If the farmers did not grow enough food, then people would go hungry the next year. To get a good crop, farmers had to keep watering the plants. Early Egyptians carried water from the river, but soon they were using ditches and ponds to make watering easier. This system of "irrigation" was carefully controlled. The farmers dug a series of deep ponds that filled with water during the inundation. The ponds fed water to the fields by a series of wide "canals" and smaller ditches. The flow of water was controlled with wooden boards. The ditches could also be filled with water from the river. Just before the inundation, farmers had to clear out any debris from the canals, ditches, and ponds. This was one of the jobs that people did as duty work for the pharaoh.

The fields were divided up by the ditches into areas that covered about five *aroura* (equivalent to about 3.3 acres). One *aroura* was the amount of land that would grow enough to feed a family. Many farmers just farmed one *aroura*, but they could farm up to ten of these patches.

▶ *This tomb model shows a farmer plowing. Farm tools were wooden and could not have been easy to use for plowing heavy soil. But the soil produced by the Nile mud was very fertile and easy to plow.*

Most of the farmland was used to grow grain, mainly barley and emmer (a kind of wheat). The farmers grew vegetables such as leeks, onions, garlic, beans, lentils, lettuce, and cucumbers. But grain was the most important crop. It was used to make bread and beer, which were two of the most important parts of the ancient Egyptian diet.

The farmers also raised animals. Oxen were kept for plowing, sheep for their wool. Both of these animals were also useful for milk and meat. Goats, geese, and ducks were also raised. Taking care of the animals was usually a job for the children of farming families.

▲ A map showing how closely Egyptian farming was linked to the Nile. It also shows that farmers worked on the land closest to towns and cities.

When the Nile started to rise for the inundation, the scribes watched the water level carefully. They had special gauges set up along the Nile, and the scribes kept careful records of how far and how fast the river rose each year. Thus they were able to tell how much land would flood. Too little flooding and people would not have enough to eat. Too high a rise in water level and people would have to pack up and flee because their homes would become flooded!

▼ *This decorated slate, called the Battlefield Palette, comes from early Egypt. It was made to celebrate the victories of King Narmer. Here, captured enemies are being led back to Egypt to work as slaves or to be killed by the king.*

Slaves

It is hard to tell how many slaves there were in ancient Egypt. Some people were bought and sold as if they were property. There were also many Egyptians who lived hard lives that people today would probably consider to be as bad as slavery.

Being a slave could be a terrible life. Slaves often got the worst jobs and could be beaten, starved, and badly treated in other ways. On the other hand, some slaves seem to have had good lives. They were treated as part of the family, especially in homes where there were only one or two slaves. They worked hard but were treated fairly. Often, childless couples freed and then adopted family slaves. A family with no sons might free a male slave and then marry him to their daughter.

▲ Servants were often given hard work in the fields or mines. These workers are pressing grapes for winemaking. There were many Egyptian servants. Only foreigners could become slaves.

A slave could thus become a part of Egyptian society and even end up running his own business.

Many Egyptians worked for a particular landowner. They could not leave his estate on their own, but he could send them to work for other people if he wanted to. Other Egyptians were punished for crimes, or for avoiding doing their duty work, by being sent to do forced work for a set time. This was usually on royal land or in the mines. Sometimes a criminal's wife and children had to do forced labor, too, as part of his punishment. If his crimes were bad enough, his children inherited the punishment after his death.

Slaves were the least important people in Egyptian society, so there is very little written about them. But because they were "property," we can find out things about them from people's wills, which dispose of slaves with other property. Here are some examples: "I leave my wife everything that my brother, Ankhreni, gave me. She can give it to any of the children that she and I have had together. I also give her the three slaves that my brother left to me. She can give them to one of my children, too." (Will of Wah, a priest, 1506 BCE) "As for the slave belonging to me called Amenuiy, who I captured while following the ruler, I give him to Takemet, the daughter of my sister, as husband. He will not be without wealth." (Will of Sabastet, the king's hairdresser, 1506 BCE)

Relations with Other Countries

Generally, ancient Egyptians dealt with foreign countries in two ways. They either fought with them or traded with them, depending upon which country was stronger. When Egypt was weak, other countries threatened to invade, hoping to take control. When Egypt was strong, the pharaohs regained control of any land that had been lost in times of weakness.

The Egyptian army was very organized, with the pharaoh as chief war leader. The army had foot soldiers and men in war chariots. There was also a navy. Soldiers and sailors who were brave were usually given medals and promotions. Any enemies the Egyptians captured became slaves.

The ancient Egyptians were well placed to trade with other countries. There was nothing that they had to import because they were self-sufficient.

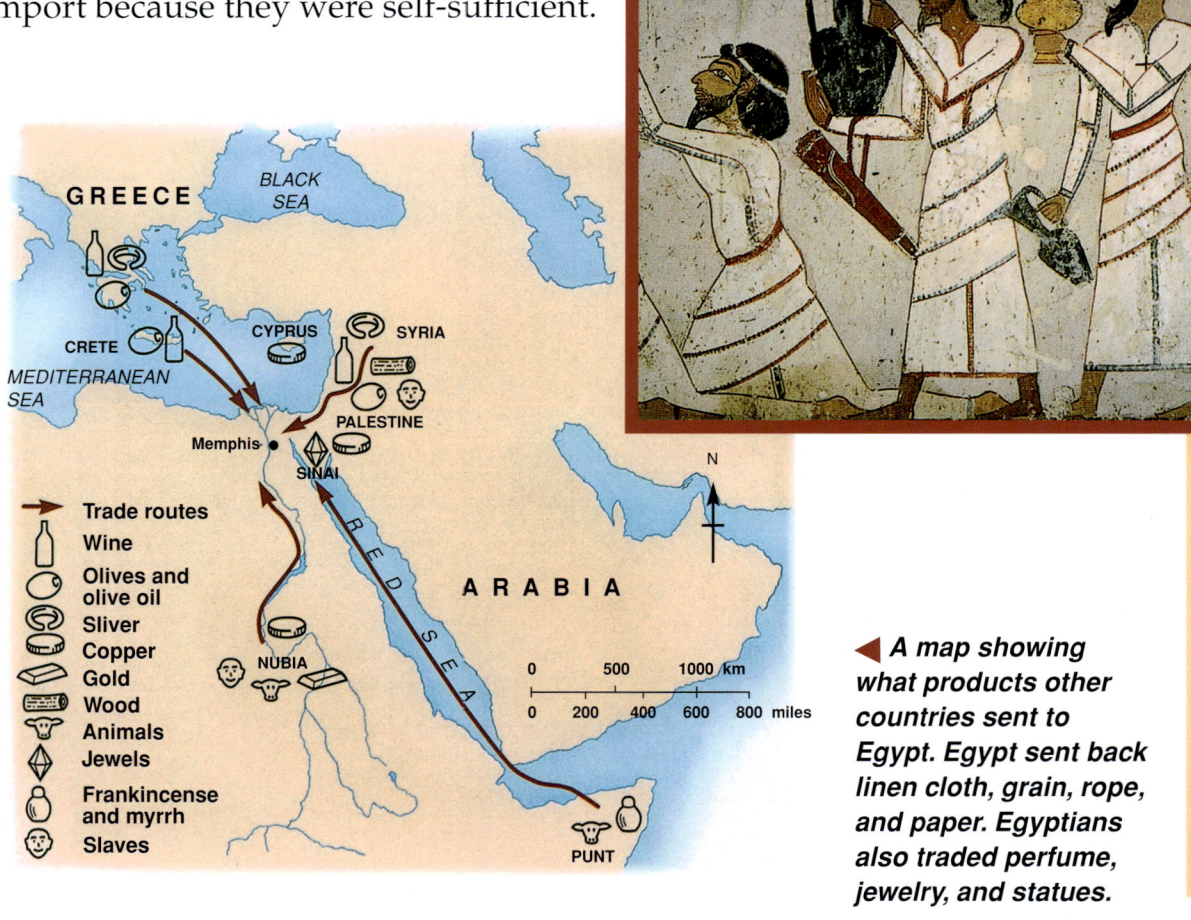

▼ This painting, from the tomb of Sobekhotep, from about 1400 BCE, shows Syrian ambassadors bringing presents to the pharaoh.

◀ A map showing what products other countries sent to Egypt. Egypt sent back linen cloth, grain, rope, and paper. Egyptians also traded perfume, jewelry, and statues.

On the other hand, they had lots of things that other people wanted, such as gold and semi-precious stones. They had to import silver, and so it was seen as more precious than gold.

The Egyptians had most contact with Nubia, upriver, to the south. Nubia was weaker than Egypt much of the time, so it could be exploited. Asia, to the east, had no river route to Egypt. First contact was made by nomads, across the desert. At first, Egyptians mostly traded with Asians, but they also fought with them. The people of Asia invaded Egypt when the Middle Kingdom collapsed. Egypt grew strong again in the New Kingdom and invaded Asia. There was not much contact with the Mediterranean until 1550 BCE.

▲ *A tomb model showing an infantry regiment from the Middle Kingdom.*

This is part of a soldier's life story carved in his tomb, from about 1550 BCE. (The Egyptians cut off one hand of each of the enemy dead and counted them to keep track of the number of enemies they had killed.)

"My father was a soldier, and so I became a soldier, too. I got promoted and so could set up a household. I ran alongside the king while he rode in his chariot. While we were besieging an enemy town I showed bravery in front of the king. I got promoted. I also cut off the hand of an enemy in battle, and got a medal. In the next battle I cut off a hand and got another medal. I also captured a prisoner, so he became my slave. After the king had destroyed the Asiatics, he went south to attack the Nubians. He made a great slaughter of Nubian bowmen, and I came away with three hands and another medal."

Religion and Ritual

What Did People Believe In?

The ancient Egyptians believed in many gods and goddesses. Just like the people of Egypt, each god had a different job to do. The ancient Egyptians believed that the gods could, and did, control life in Egypt. Because they believed this, magic was an accepted part of everyday life. Egyptian doctors used herbal cures and practical medicine for setting bones and for performing surgery. Sometimes they were required to use a spell at the same time as giving the medicine. Ordinary people could use magic and prayers to the gods. They went to temples at special times for special religious ceremonies; but for everyday worship, there was a shrine in each house (usually for gods of the family such as Bes), and small outdoor shrines to other gods that people could go to at any time.

▼ These small magic charms are called amulets. These amulets show the crocodile god, Sobek. Most amulets show a god in its animal form. Each god had a special job. Bes looked after the home and children. Hapi controlled the rise and fall of the Nile. Many gods had more than one shape and name and more than one job. The most important god was the sun god. He could be shown as a scarab beetle or as a hawk with a sun on his head. He was called Re, Atum, or Khepri.

▲ This is the heart scarab of Ptahemheb. It is an amulet that was put on the breast of a mummy.

Some gods and goddesses were worshiped all over Egypt. Other gods were important in certain places and hardly heard of in others. Some gods had shrines in places that were relevant to the function of the god—there were shrines to the crocodile god, Sobek, at dangerous places on the Nile. Many gods were shown in pictures and statues as having human bodies and animal heads. Horus is the hawk-headed god, and Anubis, god of the Dead, has the head of a jackal. Osiris, one of the most important gods, is usually shown with a human face. He is always in all white (to suggest mummy bandages), and his face is often green.

Many ancient Egyptian stories were about the gods. One about the creation of the world explains how the most important gods were related. They seem to have been constantly squabbling:
"In the beginning there was nothing but water. The sun god, Atem, appeared. First he made a mud bank to stand on. Then he made Shu, god of Air, and Tefnut, goddess of Moisture. Shu and Tefnut made Geb, god of Earth, and Nut, goddess of Sky. Geb and Nut had five children. They were Osiris, Horus, Seth, Isis, and Nephythis. Isis was sister and wife of Osiris. Nephythis was wife and sister to Seth. Seth and Osiris struggled for power over Egypt. Seth held a feast and tricked Osiris into lying in a coffin. He nailed him up in it and threw the coffin into the river. Isis went to find the coffin. After much journeying and lamenting, she found the coffin, but Seth took it, chopped Osiris into pieces, and threw the bits of the body into the river. Isis carefully collected them and put them back together. This was when the real trouble began."

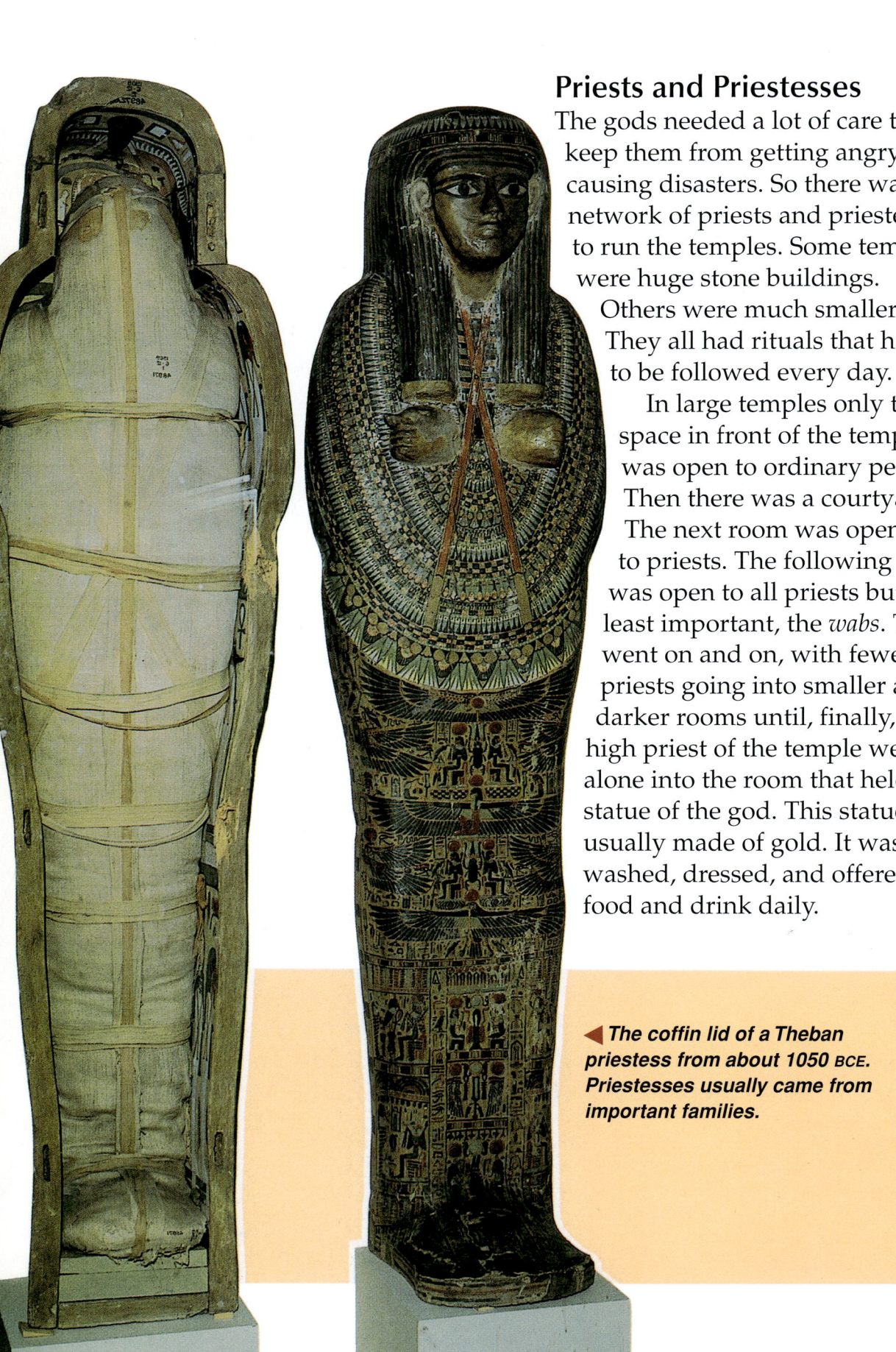

Priests and Priestesses

The gods needed a lot of care to keep them from getting angry and causing disasters. So there was a network of priests and priestesses to run the temples. Some temples were huge stone buildings. Others were much smaller. They all had rituals that had to be followed every day.

In large temples only the space in front of the temple was open to ordinary people. Then there was a courtyard. The next room was open only to priests. The following room was open to all priests but the least important, the *wabs*. This went on and on, with fewer priests going into smaller and darker rooms until, finally, the high priest of the temple went alone into the room that held the statue of the god. This statue was usually made of gold. It was washed, dressed, and offered food and drink daily.

◀ **The coffin lid of a Theban priestess from about 1050 BCE. Priestesses usually came from important families.**

On special occasions the statue was taken out of the shrine at the center of the temple and carried in a procession for all the people to see as it passed by.

There were far fewer priestesses than priests, and most of these served the goddess Hathor. A few were allowed to serve other gods, but they usually did not serve male gods, except as temple musicians; High priestesses were an exception. They could serve the most important gods. There were very few high priestesses.

In the Old Kingdom, the job of priest or priestess was only part-time. There were very few public ceremonies, just daily rituals, which were organized so that priests worked one month out of three. By the time of the New Kingdom, there were more festivals and ceremonies to arrange. The most important priests found that their work became full time. There were more of the less important priests, so they could still combine other jobs with their priestly duties.

▲ This painting on papyrus shows the burial of the royal scribe, Hunefer. The mummy of Hunefer is held up by a priest in a jackal mask, representing the god Anubis. Another priest (wearing a leopard skin) makes offerings to the gods while two other priests perform rituals. The women family members are mourning.

The Greek historian Herodotus wrote this description of Egyptian priests after he visited Egypt in about 450 BCE: "The Egyptians are more religious than any other nation in the world. They are all clean in their habits, but the priests especially so. Priests shave their bodies completely every other day, to keep themselves free from lice. They wear only linen and shoes made from the papyrus plant. They wash in cold water twice a day and every night. They are not allowed to eat pork, fish, or beans."

Mummies

The Egyptians believed that the spirits of the dead left their bodies but would come back to use them again in the future. So it was important to keep dead bodies in the best possible condition.

Preserving your relatives' bodies was important. You would meet them in the afterlife, and you would have to answer to them if you had failed in your duty.

▼ **Early burials left the bodies unwrapped, so the sand would dry them out. The bodies were curled up inside baskets made of reeds.**

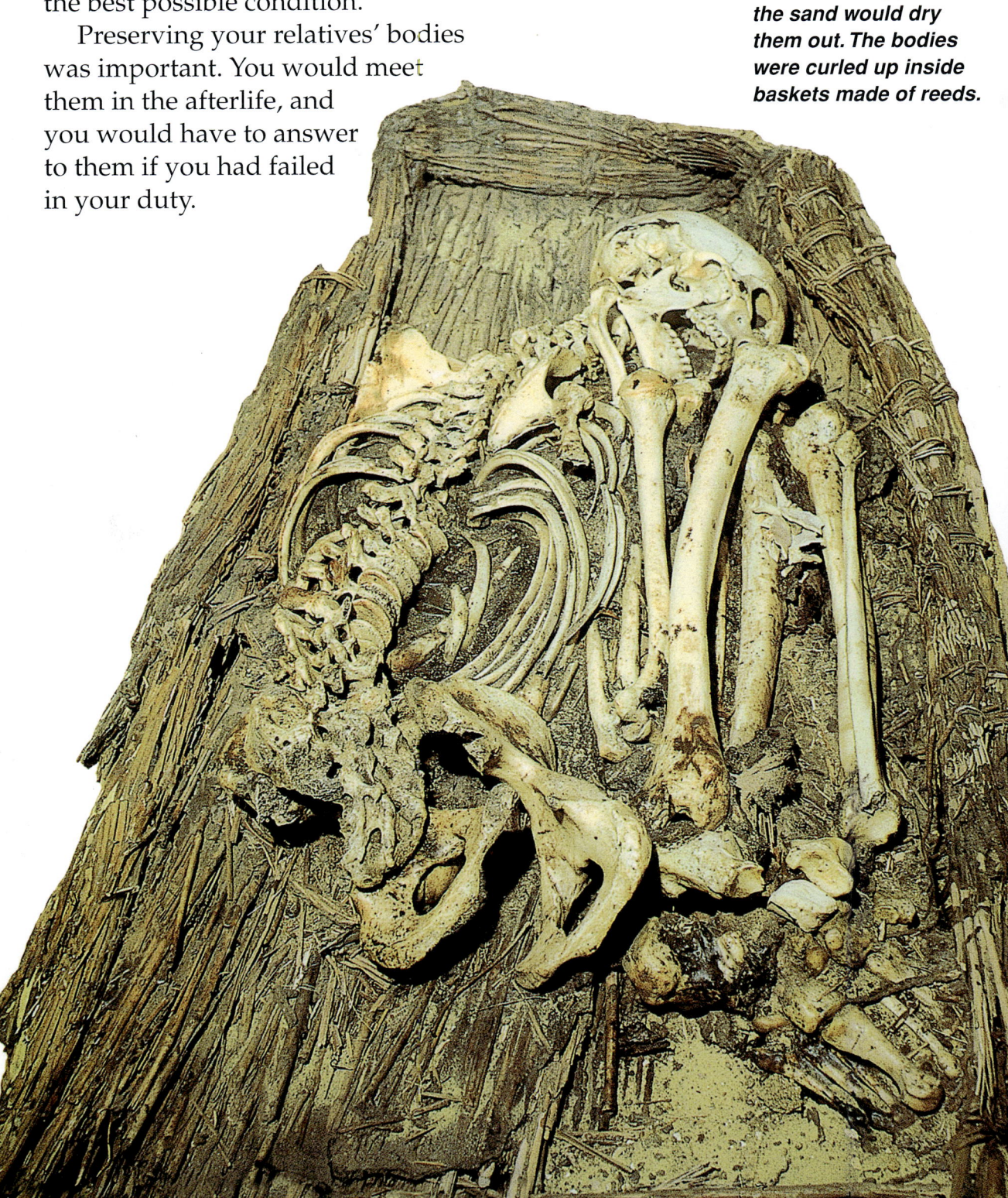

The first Egyptians buried their dead in a curled up position, either directly into the hot sand (which dried them out and preserved them naturally) or into the sand in baskets. Later they began to bury people lying out straight, in wooden sarcophagi (coffins). As soon as the bodies were out of contact with the sand, they were no longer naturally preserved. They began to rot. So the Egyptians learned how to preserve the bodies by embalming them and making them into mummies. From the Old Kingdom onward, preserving dead bodies was a job separate from the work of the priests in burying the dead. The body was washed and purified and laid out on a bed of natron (a kind of salt) to dry out. Then it was wrapped and left in the tomb.

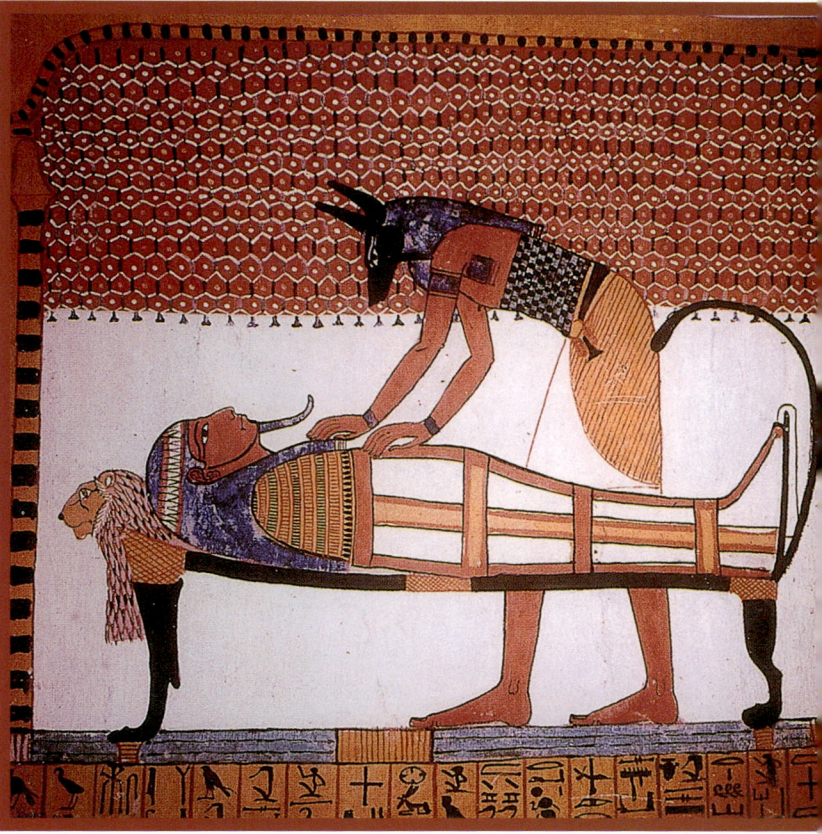

▲ This tomb painting shows the process of mummification. Anubis, the guardian of tombs and the god of the dead, is the embalmer, bending over the mummy.

In 1975, a female mummy was unwrapped at Manchester Museum in England. She had been unwrapped before, in Ancient Egyptian times, about 100 years after she was first buried. The Egyptians who had unwrapped her had found that her legs and feet were broken. They had made her splints for her legs and clay and reed feet so that she could walk in the afterlife.

Embalming

Early embalmers wrapped bodies tightly in strips of linen. But the bodies rotted inside the bandages. So they removed the organs and the brain, where the rotting began. Because the dead person would need these body parts, they were preserved separately and put in special jars, called canopic jars. During the Late New Kingdom, embalmers preserved the organs, wrapped them, and packed them back into the body cavity. The body was then wrapped in linen strips—more than 3,000 sq. ft. (300 sq. m) were used on an adult. Often magic amulets were wound into the bandages. When the mummy was wrapped, an amulet showing the eye of Horus was often placed on it, to protect the body from harm.

As embalming became more complicated, so did sarcophagi. Instead of a single wooden box, embalmers used human-shaped cases that fitted inside each other. However, poor people went on burying their dead in the sand in the same way they always had.

▼ *These beautiful pots have the name of Rameses II inscribed on them. They may have been used for holding oil or some other substance necessary in the tomb.*

The Greek historian Herodotus wrote this description of embalming, after his visit to Egypt about 450 BCE: "When a body is brought to the embalmers, they show the family of the dead person samples of their skill, and tell them the prices. Then they agree what the family wants to pay. This is the most expensive process: they extract as much of the brain as possible, through the nose with an iron hook. They open the side with a flint knife and take out all the organs inside. The cavity is then washed with palm wine and then a mixture of resin and spices. Then the cavity is filled with spices and placed in natron, fully covered, for 70 days. The body is then washed and wrapped from head to foot in linen strips smeared with resin. It is then placed in a wooden box, shaped like the human figure."

Burial

There were special places for burial, usually in the desert, across the river from where people lived. They were not too far away, because relatives visited regularly with offerings of food and drink. There were tombs cut into the rock under the desert sand, with buildings where offerings of food and drink could be made to the dead.

The Burial Ceremony

The priests and the family of the dead person took the body to the burial ground, usually by boat. They went through the religious rituals that were needed to make sure that the dead person was ready for the afterlife and for the time he or she would spend in the world of the dead, waiting to be called to the afterlife. The most important of these was the "Opening of the Mouth" ceremony. A priest touched all the openings of the body (not just the mouth) with a special tool. This let the spirit out of the body and provided it with a way back in. Since the body had been embalmed by then, they did not make real openings in the body. Then the priests burned incense, said prayers, and made offerings to the gods. They made sure that the body was lying facing the rising sun. Then they shut the tomb.

It seems that most people who were not the poorest workers or slaves had tombs. Tombs were decorated with pictures showing all the things the dead would need in the afterlife. There were also religious writings, copied on scrolls, called Books of the Dead, and written on the coffins and the walls of the tomb. Food, clothes, furniture, ornaments, and tools were buried with dead people—everything they would need to live their afterlife in the same way as their "first" life. They were buried with shabtis, too. Shabtis were human figurines that were meant to do the duty work of the dead when they came back to life. Rich people were buried with lots of shabtis and pictures of their servants. But even people who were not very well-off would have a shabti to do their duty work in the fields when they died.

▲ **This is just one of the Shabtis of Sety I, from the Valley of the Kings. Sety I ruled Egypt from 1294 BCE to 1279 BCE. His body and burial goods were moved several times to keep them safe from tomb robbers.**

▶ **This wooden shabti box was for Anhai, a priestess. The picture shows Anhai, the deceased, and her soul-bird receiving water from Nut, goddess of the sycamore tree.**

The spell that was written on many shabtis was:
"Oh thou shabti! If (name of dead person) is called to work in the underworld, to plow the fields, irrigate the canals, or carry sand from east to west—now there are reasons why he cannot do his duty. If he is called, then 'Here I am,' you shall say, 'I will do it,' and do the work in the dead person's place."

Art and Architecture

Art and Literature

Most ancient Egyptian art and literature that has survived to the present day has come from tombs and temples. Many paintings and sculptures were made to accompany the dead into the afterlife. The artists who made them had to obey rules. Everything had to be as perfect as possible—including the people in the painting.

▼ Sometimes artists could break the rules. Two of these musicians are drawn facing out of the painting. But most of the time artists obeyed the rules they had been taught to follow.

Sometimes people were shown with children, but women were not shown as pregnant—pregnancy could be dangerous. The most important person in the picture was shown as bigger than others. Wives were sometimes the same size as their husbands, but this was a sign of love and respect; usually they were smaller. Servants can be mistaken for children in paintings, because they are drawn so small. Faces and bodies were shown from the side, but both shoulders were in the picture. It would be impossible to really stand like this; you would have to twist at the waist and neck in different directions!

Archaeologists have discovered some ancient Egyptian poetry, as well as stories. Some of these poems were about falling in love: "My heart thought of my love for you when half my hair was plaited; I came at a run to find you, and left my hair unfinished. Now if you let me plait my hair I will be done in a moment."

It is hard to untangle Egyptian literature from art, because the writings are full of pictures. The ancient Egyptians developed two forms of writing. The first was hieroglyphics. These were pictures used first to show whole things and then to show sounds. They were hard to draw and were often built around actual pictures. This was not something that ordinary people, or even ordinary scribes, would learn to do. So a simplified version of this, called hieratic, was used for letters, business accounts, wills, and even the recording of some stories.

▶ **This papyrus shows the hieratic script. Because it was a simplified form of hieroglyphics, hieratic script was easy to write quickly. Scribes wrote with a brush on wood or with a reed pen on papyrus.**

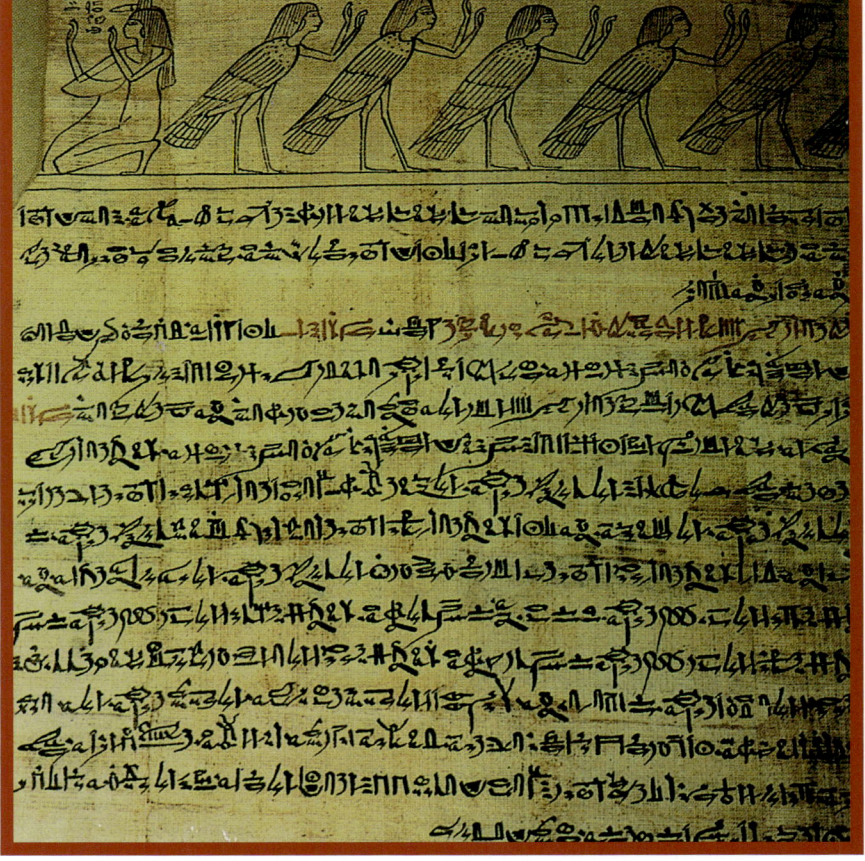

Buildings

The ancient Egyptians used two main building materials. Most buildings, including ordinary homes and less important temples, were built with mud bricks. They were well built, but wore away and had to be replaced. Important temples, tombs, and pyramids were made of stone or built into the rock that lay under the desert sand.

The stone structures that the ancient Egyptians built were often huge. They were well designed, and they took a great number of people a very long time to build. The builders had no machinery to help them. They used rollers to move the heavy blocks of stone from place to place and may have used wooden levers to move the blocks into position. They had no lifting devices like pulleys, but instead relied on huge numbers of workers. Some of the workers were people doing their duty work for the pharaoh; some of them were slaves or prisoners sent to work on building sites.

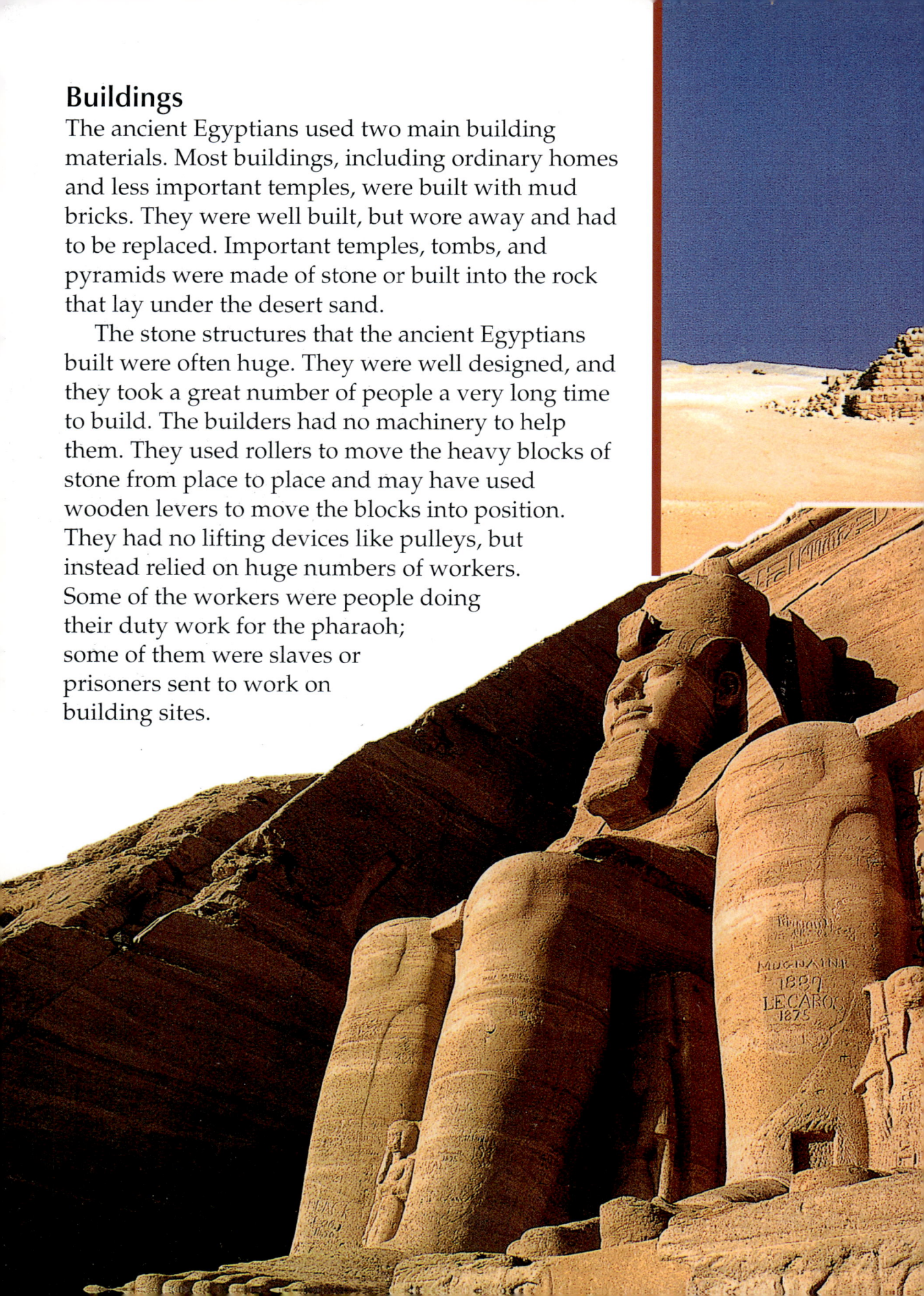

▲ **The pyramids at Giza are probably the most famous of all of the pyramids. The step-sided ones at the front of the picture are the smaller, less important pyramids, which are not very well preserved.**

◀ **In 1955, the temples of Rameses at Abu Simbel had to be moved, to make way for a new dam that was being built. Block by block, the temples were moved to a plateau above the cliff from which they had been cut.**

The pyramids were the pharaohs' tombs. The first pyramid was built in steps. The biggest pyramid is the Great Pyramid. It took about 20 years to build. The base covered an area of about 13 acres (5 ha). It was 820 ft. (250 m) high and was made of over 2.3 million limestone blocks of various sizes. The lightest weighed about 2.5 tons, the heaviest about 15 tons. About 5,000 men worked on it for most of the year, though there were more workers during the inundation. Despite the care taken to keep them from being broken into, all the pyramids had been robbed by about 1000 BCE.

Builders and Decorators

We have rare evidence about the workers on the tombs of the Valley of the Kings. A village was built at Deir-el-Medina, about 2 mi. (3 km) from the tombs, for the men and their families. Unlike settlements by the river (which have crumbled away and been built over many times), this village has survived. Archaeologists have studied the remains and documents (including accounts and work schedules), which give a picture of everyday life there. About 1500 BCE, Deir-el-Medina had about 20 houses surrounded by a wall. By 1150 BCE, it had about 70 houses inside an extended wall, with 50 more outside it. The workers who lived there were a mixture of stonemasons, carpenters, painters, and sculptors.

Deir-el-Medina was not by the river, so it did not grow any of its own food, nor did it have any available water.

▼ **The remains of Deir-el-Medina as they are today. The village was built around one long street with houses running off it. The houses usually had four small rooms.**

Food, water, and everything else the villagers needed was supplied by the government and brought in on donkeys.

The workers of the Valley of the Kings were divided into two groups, one to work on the left side of the tomb, the other to work on the right. Each group had a foreman. A scribe, who was also the villagers' priest, kept all the records and organized the foremen.

The men worked at the tombs for ten days, then had two days off at home. They had other days off, too. They did not work on feast days or when they were sick. They were given time off for reasons that ranged from extending their houses to brewing beer. The records show most workmen worked only for six months of the year, when all the days off are taken into account. They were not paid wages, but were given homes, food, and clothes.

Men and women worked and traded for themselves at Deir-el-Medina. The men used their skills to paint or provide equipment for village tombs. The women wove cloth and brewed beer. Some people hired out donkeys or servants. A lot of this was done on the basis of a simple exchange that both sides agreed was fair. So a painter might agree to paint the walls of a tomb in exchange for a coffin and some grain or the use of a donkey for a number of days.

On at least one occasion, the villagers of Deir-el-Medina stopped working and wrote a letter of complaint to the pharaoh saying: "We are hungry and thirsty. We have no clothes, no fat, no fish, and no vegetables. We write this to the King, our good lord, so that we may be given the means to live."

Everyday Life

Houses and Homes

Ancient Egyptian houses were built of mud brick, whitewashed on the inside and then painted in bright colors or with patterns and pictures. Houses were quite small, because people spent a lot of time outside. An ordinary house had an entrance room, a main living room, and smaller rooms for sleeping, working, or storing things. The smaller rooms were either all off the main room or at the back of the house.

▲ This painting from the tomb of Nebamun shows the garden of a rich man. He would probably have had a big house with beautifully decorated rooms.

◀ This tomb model is of a house with rounded doors and a staircase to a vented roof. Models like this provided a home for the soul in the afterlife. This house would have been for an ordinary family.

Rich people had bathrooms, with an area with a sloping floor where you could stand and pour water over yourself. There was also a pottery container of sand to use as a toilet. Most houses were one story high, perhaps with a cellar dug into the ground for storage. Some houses were on more than one level, with workrooms at the bottom and the main room on the next floor. People cooked outside—on the roof or in an outside courtyard. Most houses had an awning on the roof, to make a shady patch to sit in. Well-off people had gardens with ponds (to make watering easier and to keep the area cool). They grew trees for shade and fruit and vegetables to eat.

Ancient Egyptians had very little furniture. Most people had stools to sit on, although some people had low, deep chairs, with a back but no arms. Tables were small and low. People slept on mud-brick beds or on wooden bedframes that had flax straps to support the mattresses. They had linen bedding and used wooden headrests to support the neck. People stored everything in chests, which came in all shapes and sizes.

This inventory (list of contents) of a workman's house at Deir-el-Medina shows the kinds of belongings you might expect to find in the home of an ordinary person: 3 sacks of barley, 1 ½ sacks of emmer (a kind of wheat), 1 ¾ sacks of beans, 25 bunches of onions, 1 door, 2 beds, 1 chest, 2 folding stools, 1 clothes chest, 1 large filled chest, 2 bases for cooking on, 2 footstools, 2 wooden folding stools, 2 wooden serving trays, 1 reed serving tray, 1 stone pestle.

All Dressed Up

Ancient Egyptians wore clothes made of undyed, sun-bleached linen—a cloth spun from flax. The difference between the clothes of rich and poor people was not the cloth, nor the color of the cloth, but how much cloth they wore and how thin and soft it was. Poor people wore thick linen. The rich wore linen spun so fine that you could almost see through it.

Clothes changed with fashion and became more complicated as time went on. In the Old Kingdom, most men wore a sort of kilt wrapped around and tied at the waist. In cold weather they wore cloaks. Poor men wore only loincloths. Women wore long shifts. In the Middle Kingdom the fashion was to wear pleated linen.

By the New Kingdom people wanted pleats and fringes. They wore layers of clothes, and men began to wear tunics as well as kilts.

On their feet, people wore sandals made of grass, reeds, or leather. Most, but not all, men and women shaved their heads or wore their hair very short, to keep cool. They wore wigs, made from human hair, which sometimes still had the hair lice in them from the original owner.

Ancient Egyptian men and women both wore jewelry. They shaved their bodies to avoid lice and oiled them to protect themselves against the weather. They wore perfumed oils, too. Men and women wore makeup. They outlined their eyes with black or green eyepaint. The black eyepaint, kohl, was also used as part of eye treatments by doctors and may have helped against the glare of the sun. Ancient Egyptians also used red ocher powder mixed with fat to color their cheeks and lips.

▲ *A linen blouse, thought to be one of the earliest garments in the world, from 3100 BCE. Considering that they had only very simple spinning and weaving equipment, Egyptian cloth was remarkably finely woven and smooth.*

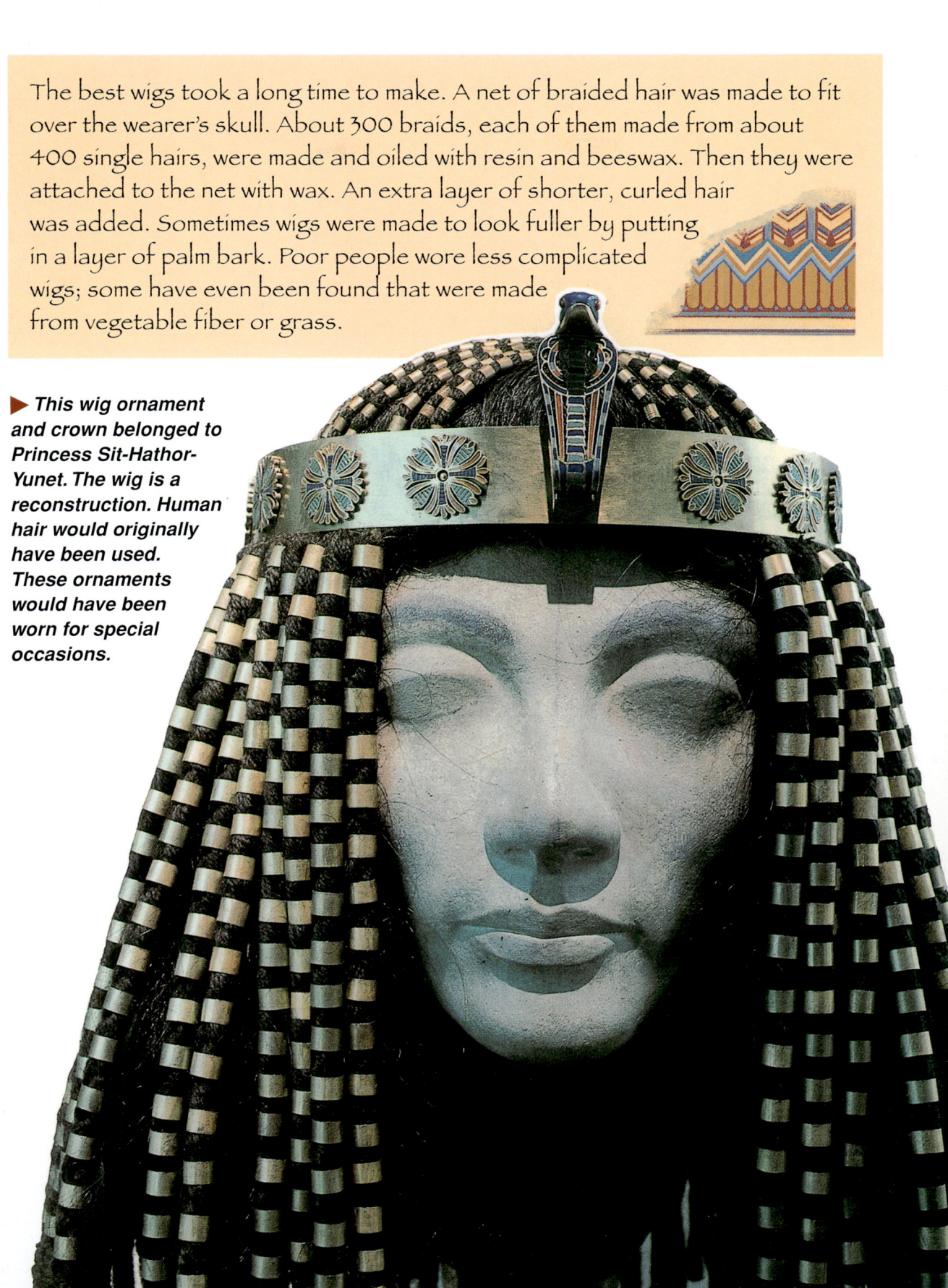

The best wigs took a long time to make. A net of braided hair was made to fit over the wearer's skull. About 300 braids, each of them made from about 400 single hairs, were made and oiled with resin and beeswax. Then they were attached to the net with wax. An extra layer of shorter, curled hair was added. Sometimes wigs were made to look fuller by putting in a layer of palm bark. Poor people wore less complicated wigs; some have even been found that were made from vegetable fiber or grass.

▶ **This wig ornament and crown belonged to Princess Sit-Hathor-Yunet. The wig is a reconstruction. Human hair would originally have been used. These ornaments would have been worn for special occasions.**

Food and Feasting

The ancient Egyptians ate a wide variety of foods. We do not know exactly when they ate their meals, but they probably ate three meals a day, with their main meal in the cool of the evening. Most people ate lots of bread, which was coarse-grained and had sand and grit in it. This wore their teeth down and gave them a lot of trouble with tooth decay.

Besides bread, ordinary people ate lots of vegetables: onions, leeks, garlic, cucumber, lettuce, and beans. They also ate lots of fruit: grapes, figs, pomegranates, and dates. Dates were used to sweeten things, as was honey—the ancient Egyptians were the first people to keep bees rather than just collecting wild honey. Ordinary people did not eat meat or fish every day, although they ate them from time to time. They mostly drank beer. People of higher rank ate and drank the same things as the poor, although they ate meat and fish much more often and drank wine, too.

▼ *Food was among the important things that the Egyptians left for their dead. Early Egyptians buried their dead with a few belongings and pots of food, as in the picture below. Later on, burials were more complicated; there were also temples at burial places, where offerings of food could be left for dead relatives.*

▶ *An Egyptian wall painting of a feast, from the tomb of Nebamun at Thebes, shows servants bringing the well-dressed guests food.*

Wealthy Egyptian citizens held feasts and parties in the evening. There was lots of food and drink and music and entertainment. At feasts there was a much greater choice of food than at ordinary meals. There would be many different kinds of meat: beef, lamb, goat, goose, and duck. There would also be many different kinds of fish, vegetables, bread, cakes, and fruit. People sat in the biggest room of the house on a collection of chairs, stools, folding stools, and cushions, eating the food from small, low tables. They wore their best clothes and wigs. Wall paintings of parties show people with strangely colored cones on the top of their heads. These were cones of fat that had been mixed with perfume. The fat melted in the heat of the party and ran down into the wig of the person wearing it, giving off a lovely smell.

Many of the herbs and plants that the ancient Egyptians grew were also used in medicine. The Egyptians used cucumber, lettuce, and herbs in their medicines. They used willow bark as a painkiller—scientists have discovered that there is a chemical in willow bark that is the same as the chemical used in aspirin today.

You could eat and drink out, as well as at home, in ancient Egypt. One of the books of advice for people on how to behave has this to say about drinking in taverns: "Do not get drunk in the taverns in which they drink beer, for fear that people repeat words which have left your mouth without your knowing you have said them."

▼ **This is a tomb statue of Seneb the dwarf and his family, from about 2300 BCE. Seneb and his wife, Senetites, had two children—a boy and a girl. The boy is the darker skinned of the two children with a lock of hair on the side of his head.**

Family Life

Family life was very important to the ancient Egyptians. We know that they did not have special marriage ceremonies, but we do know that there was some celebration of the marriage. A man and woman were considered to be married from the time they set up house together. The family consisted of everyone who lived in the home—parents, children, grandparents, servants, and slaves. People were encouraged to marry early and start a family. They could get divorced by simply agreeing to part and ceasing to live in the same house. This meant that there were second, even third marriages.

Dividing the property of a dead person who had been married several times could get very complicated! This does not mean that people did not treat getting married seriously. There were many people who married only once and remained happily married.

Women were seen as equal to men in some ways. They could own their own property, including slaves, and they could buy and sell things in their own names. They were seen as different from men—there were certain kinds of work they were not allowed to do.

▲ The scribe, Ani, and his wife, Tutu, playing the board game called Senet. Two players raced each other to be the first to reach the Kingdom of Osiris. This is an illustration from the Book of the Dead made for the scribe's burial about 1200 BCE.

Washing clothes—a female task in many societies—was done by men in ancient Egypt, possibly because the washing was done in the crocodile-infested Nile River. Women were not supposed to do work that involved using cutting tools, including preparing and cooking meat. Work that women did included grinding corn, baking, and spinning and weaving cloth. They also made wigs and perfume, and worked as servants, entertainers, and priestesses.

Most entertainers and musicians were women. They played pipes, stringed instruments something like a harp, and cymbals. Temple musicians also played a sistrum (a handheld rattle) that was used in rituals. Besides playing music, women entertainers danced, sang, and performed acrobatics. The ancient Egyptians probably passed on their musical skills without writing down the music; certainly no written music has been discovered yet. This means that we do not know what kinds of music they enjoyed.

Women and Children

The ancient Egyptians thought that the most important thing a woman could do was to marry and have children. One of the main reasons for divorce in ancient Egypt seems to have been the wife's inability to have children. Male children were important to society in ancient Egypt because fathers taught their trades to their sons, who then inherited their property. For society to thrive, all trades had to keep going. So, couples who could not have children would adopt a son, either an orphan or a slave—often someone who had worked for the family. Children were also important because they arranged their parents' burials. It was important to be buried properly, so it was important to have children who would feel responsible for making sure that everything was done right.

Childhood was short in ancient Egypt. Girls helped their mothers around the house as soon as they were able to, and boys began to learn their trade from their fathers at an early age. They began by running errands and doing the easy jobs, such as scaring birds off the fields or sweeping out the workshop, and they moved on to more difficult jobs as they grew older. This sounds as if children had very little fun. But much of their early work was almost play, part of family life, helping their parents, and feeling grown up. They were given plenty of time for play, too. Tomb paintings show children playing leapfrog and tug-of-war and racing each other.

Children were told lots of stories. Many stories were about Egypt and had morals, to teach the children how to behave. Other stories were about far-off lands. These stories often said how much better it was to live in Egypt than anywhere else.

◀ *A wooden, paddle-shaped doll from about 1900 BCE. This doll was not for children. Adults would keep it as a good-luck charm to bring them fertility so they could have children.*

Books on how to behave were full of advice about marriage and family life. Here are some examples: "Take a wife while you are young, that she will make a son for you. She should have your children while you are both young. It is proper to make people." (i.e., to have children).

"Do not try to control your wife and tell her what to do in the house, if she is efficient. Do not say to her 'Where is it? Get it!' when things are in their right place. Watch her with joy. Avoid trouble at home, and it will not start."

"Instructing a woman is like putting sand into a split sack."

"Do not tell your wife secrets, for what you have said to her will go out into the street when she does!"

"Let your wife see your wealth, but do not trust her with it."

▼ *Children playing games. The "living merry-go-round" was formed by girls swinging each other around in a circle, and "Hathor's dancing game" involved dancing with mirrors and hand-shaped rattles.*

Egypt in Decline

Divisions and Decline

The last pharaoh of the New Kingdom, Rameses XI, died about 1070 BCE. After the death of Rameses III, 100 years earlier, there were eight pharaohs with less and less of a grip on the country. Now the kingdom was divided into two. The northern part was run by kings based at Tanis, in the Delta. The southern part was run by the high priests of Thebes. When the kingdom broke up 300 years later, other countries began to think of invasion. The Nubians invaded first, about 724 BCE. They were followed by the Persians in 525 BCE, and the Greeks in 332 BCE. The Egyptians welcomed the Greeks, whom they saw as rescuing their country from Persian rule. The Greek rulers, the Ptolemies, were careful to act as if they were preserving traditional Egyptian ways, even when they were changing them.

As the Roman Empire rose to power, the Egyptian kings tried to become independent allies of Rome. They failed, and in 30 BCE, when Queen Cleopatra died, Egypt was absorbed into the Roman Empire. It remained under Roman rule, converting to Christianity when Rome did.

▲ *Archers shown on a wall painting at the Palace of Artaxerxes, king of Persia, built about 420 BCE. The Persian kings ruled Egypt for most of the years from about 525 BCE to about 332 BCE.*

Cleopatra was the last of the Greek rulers of Egypt. She was born about 68 BCE and became queen at the age of 17. She ruled jointly with her brother, Ptolemy, until 49 BCE, when he threw her out and tried to rule alone. She asked the Romans for help, and Julius Caesar brought an army to put her back on the throne. Her brother was killed and she was made queen, ruling jointly with her younger brother (also, confusingly, called Ptolemy). She lived with Julius Caesar until he was assassinated in 44 BCE. In 31 BCE, the Romans declared war on Egypt, partly as a result of her plotting against them. When it became clear that the Romans would win, Cleopatra committed suicide.

As the power of Rome declined, its empire began to fall apart. Egypt was taken over by Arabs in 640 CE. Eventually the Turks took over. It was not until the 1960s that Egypt was ruled by Egyptians again.

How did all these various invasions affect Egypt? One of the biggest effects was that Egypt was no longer so self-contained. When Egypt was a separate country, it was able, most of the time, to choose whether to get involved with other countries or not—either through war or trade. Once Egypt was part of the lands held by other countries, it became involved in their business, to varying degrees. Once there was a mixing of ideas and ways of life, the period that we call "ancient Egypt" came to an end. But the Egyptians did not suddenly vanish. Nor did their way of life change suddenly and dramatically with each invasion.

Alexander the Great drove the Persians out of Egypt, and he was welcomed by the Egyptians. He took over as pharaoh, and this statue shows him with a pharaoh's headdress. He was careful not to try to change Egyptian ways.

Influences on Egypt

From the invading cultures, the Egyptians took things that suited them—big ideas (such as Christianity) and small ideas (such as Greek pens, which worked better than Egyptian pens). They usually mixed new and old ideas. For instance, statues of the god Bes from Roman times show the old god in Roman armor. Egyptians began to trade more with other countries, so they used money instead of bartering or using a standard metal weight. Under the Ptolemies, they went on to develop the most organized state bank system in the Empire.

The first lighthouse was built in Egypt, under the Ptolemies. It was designed by a Greek architect and built by Egyptians. It became one of the Seven Wonders of the ancient world (ancient Egypt contributed another of these wonders—the pyramids).

> The Greek historian Herodotus wrote this after a visit to Egypt about 450 BCE: "The Egyptians are unwilling to adopt Greek customs, or, to speak more generally, the customs of any other country. I know of just one exception: at Chemmis, near Thebes, they have built a temple to Perseus which is very grand. They have done this because they believe it is the place where he was born."

▶ *These two Roman mummies contain the bodies of children. The Romans were always happy to let various parts of their empire keep their old ways, as long as they did not interfere with the way the Romans wanted to run the country. These mummies show the mixture of classical Roman and Egyptian culture. The embalming is Egyptian; the portraits are classical.*

▲ This relief of the Roman Emperor Augustus shows him dressed as a pharaoh and making an offering to the Egyptian god, Isis. Until they became Christians, the Romans would happily accept the gods of countries that they conquered into their own system. It helped the countries they took over to accept their rule.

The Legacy of Egypt

What Remains?

The ancient Egyptians lived a long time ago. When people talk about the legacy of the Egyptians, they often mean the pyramids and tombs along the Nile or perhaps the mummies and other artifacts that have survived from the time and can be seen in museums. But you don't have to go to Egypt, or to a museum, to be reminded of the Egyptians. Many things from ancient Egypt are still familiar to us today.

The Egyptians were among the first people to use calendars. Their year was divided into 12 months, made up of 365 days—just like ours. They measured time the way we do, although people argue over whether our calendar comes from theirs. It certainly shows that they thought about time as we do; other ancient civilizations measured time very differently. The Egyptians had clocks to measure the hours, too: water clocks and shadow clocks that were very early sundials. Water clocks became popular throughout the ancient world as a way of telling time.

▲ *A copy of a book of mathematics called the Rhind Papyrus. It has a series of problems on figuring out areas, measuring angles, and calculating volume.*

Whenever you go out in the rain, remember that the umbrella was used as a sunshade by the wealthier Egyptians. Egypt was one of the first civilizations to develop what were later called parasols, but it was not until the eighteenth century that the umbrella was brought to Europe from China.

The ancient Egyptians wrote the story about a mummy that com "A scribe steals a magical pap but is drowned by the god of writing, Thoth, for doing so. He is mummified, and the scroll is buried with him. A priest and magician, Khaemwas, breaks into the tomb to steal the papyrus. The mummy rises to stop him and agrees that they will play a game of Senet to decide who gets the scroll. The mummy wins, but Khaemwas steals the scroll anyway. He then has nothing but bad luck until he takes the scroll back and seals the tomb."

◀ This water clock, from the temple of Karnak, dates from about 1415 BCE. As the water flowed out of a reed bung in a hole near the base of the clock, the drop in the water level in the vessel showed how much time had passed.

The ancient Egyptians were probably the first people in the world to practice medicine. One papyrus that was found deals with the treatment of physical injuries. It recommends using splints, casts, and sutures to mend broken limbs and to heal wounds. These methods are very similar to those of modern medicine.

The ancient Egyptians also influenced modern art and architecture. Buildings are still decorated in the Egyptian style; there is even a pyramid-shaped skyscraper in San Francisco. All these examples prove that Egypt was one of the earliest civilizations to have such an advanced culture. It is hard to imagine such a civilization existing 5,000 years ago—Egypt even seemed ancient to the ancient Greeks! Egypt is amazing not only for its achievements but also for the length of time that the culture survived. For over 2,500 years, ancient Egypt flourished, and even today it is one of the most studied and respected civilizations in history.

▼ This man is driving cattle around a shaduf (a device for bringing water out of the river) in twentieth-century Egypt. In modern Egypt, many of the ways of life of the ancient Egyptians still live on.

Timeline

All dates are BCE

700,000 There were nomads traveling in Egypt, but no settled groups of people.
250,000 First settlements along the Nile River—mostly hunting and fishing camps.
12,000 People were living in settlements, growing crops.
6000 Bigger settlement groups; people were raising animals and making tools and pottery.
4500 Upper and Lower Egyptian groups were developing in different ways.
3500 People of Lower Egypt were building houses, perhaps even trading with other countries.
3100 Lower and Upper Egypt united by Narmer, who ruled both from Memphis.

2649–2150 OLD KINGDOM.
2650–2400 Pyramids were built as the tombs of the pharaohs.

2134–1783 MIDDLE KINGDOM.
2133 Instead of Memphis, Thebes was made the capital of Egypt.
1991–1786 Period of expanding settlement along the Nile beyond the first cataract toward Nubia. Also strengthening of hold on Sinai with copper mining there.

1550–1070 NEW KINGDOM.
1353–35 Akhenaten ruled Egypt, set up a new religion, and a new capital city, El-Amarna.
724 Nubians took over parts of Egypt.

661–333 LATE PERIOD.
525 Persians invaded Egypt.
332 Greeks invaded Egypt, led by Alexander the Great.

He was seen as a savior from Persian rule and welcomed.
30 Egypt taken into the Roman Empire on the death of the Egyptian Queen Cleopatra, who had ruled with Roman help.

Glossary

Amulet A small ornament, worn to protect a person from evil or to bring good luck.
Artifact Something that a person has made.
Awning A fabric cover used outdoors as a temporary roof.
Barter To swap something you do not need for something you want.
Book of the Dead Texts to protect and guide the dead on their journey to the afterlife.
Canopic jars Special jars used to hold the inside organs of a person who was being embalmed.
Civil war A war between people in the same country.
Complexes A collection of buildings that are all part of the same group.
Deben A set weight of metal, used instead of money in ancient Egypt.
Delta A fertile area between Cairo and the Mediterranean, also called Lower Egypt.
Fertile Very rich and full of nutrients; producing good crops.
Funerary offerings Food and drink (generally alcoholic) provided for the dead and put in their tombs.

Hieratic writing A simpler version of hieroglyphics.
Hieroglyphics A system of writing that used pictures rather than letters to show sounds or whole words.
Intermediate periods Short periods of confusion in Egypt's history when it was split and ruled by different kings at the same time.
Inundation The yearly flooding of the Nile.
Irrigation Supplying land with water using channels and ditches.
Mummy An embalmed body.
Natron A type of salt that could be dug out of the ground in certain parts of Egypt. It was used to preserve bodies.
Palette A flat stone often shaped in the form of a fish or animal. Palettes were used as grinding stones and in religious rituals.
Papyrus A reed that grew in swamps along the Nile. The young shoots were eaten. The stems of older plants were used to make boats; the tough, inside pith was beaten flat into long sheets to write on.
Pharaoh A king of Egypt.

Relief A carving in which the figures stand out from the surface of stone.
Ritual A religious action or set of actions.
Sarcophagus A stone or wooden coffin. The name means "flesh eater."
Scroll Several sheets of writing papyrus joined to make a long sheet for continuous writing.
Senet An Egyptian board game where two people race to be the first to reach the Kingdom of Osiris.
Shabti A statuette placed in tombs to do the work of the dead in the afterlife.
Shrine A place where the image of a god is placed so that people can pray to the god there.
Skyscraper A very tall building.
Step pyramid A pyramid built in layers, with sides that look like giant steps instead of being smooth.
Taverns Places that sell food and drinks to customers.
Temple A place where priests worship a god.
Valley of the Kings West of Luxor, the place where the tombs of the New Kingdom kings and their families were built.

Further Reading and Web Sites

Books
Ancient Egyptian Civilization
by Michael Bell
Rosen Central, 2009

The Egyptians: Life in Ancient Egypt
by Liz Sonneborn
Millbrook Press, 2009

Understanding People in the Past: The Ancient Egyptians
by Rosemary Rees
Heinemann-Raintree, 2007

Web Sites

http://egypt.mrdonn.org/index.html

http://www.historyforkids.org/learn/egypt/index.htm

Index

Numbers in bold are illustrations

Afterlife 10, 33, 36, 38, 45, 62
Agriculture 8–9, 11, 22–23, 61
Amulets **28**, 28–29, 34, 62
Animals 8, 10, **14**, 14, 19, 23, 28, 29, 61
Architecture 60
Army 26, 55
Art 38, 39, 60

Buildings 35, 40–41, 42, 60, 62
Burial 6, 11, **31**, 31, 32, **33**, 33, 34–35, 36–37, 51, 52

Children 14, 23, 28, 29, 38, 52, 53
Christianity 54, 56
Cleopatra 54–55
Clothes 17, 21, 31, 36, 43, 45, **46**, 46, 49, 51
Crafts 11, 12, 15, 20, 21, 38–39, 43

Desert 4, 5, 6, 9, 10, 13, 27, 16, 35, 40

Embalmers 20, 33, 34–35, 36

Families 16, 50, 53
Farming 5, 6, 8, 9, 11, 19, 22, 23
Feasts 25, 43, 49
Food 11, 15, 22–23, 31, 35, 36, 42, 45, **48**, 48, 49

Games 9, 9, 52, **53**, 53, 59
Gods and goddesses 14, 17, 20, 28, 29, 31, 36, 56, 57, 59, 63
Government 14, 15, 16, 18, 19, 21, 43
Greeks 54, 55, 56, 61

Hieratic writing 39
Hieroglyphics 18, 39, 62

Houses 9, 11, 20, 43, **44**, 44–45, 49, 50, 52, 61

Intermediate Periods 12, 13, 62, 64

Jewelry 9, **11**, 11, 15, **21**, 20–21, 46

Kings
 of Egypt 12, 13, 16, 17, 40, 41, 54, 62–63
 of Persia 54

Literature 38, 39

Magic 28, 34
Makeup 9, 20
Markets 15, 21
Marriage 50, 52–53
Medicine 28, 49
Memphis 10, 16, 62
Mining 7, 8, 11, 61
Money 21, 56, 62
Mummies 17, 20, 29, 31, **32**, 32, 33, 34–35, **56–57**, 56–57, 59, 60, 62
Music 31, 36, **38**, 38, 49, 51, 53

Nile River 4, 5, 5, 6, 8, 10, 13, 23, 23, 28, 29, 42, 51, 58, 61
Nomads 8, 27, 61
Nubia 27, 54, 61

Paintings 19, 27, 38, 38, **45**, 45, 49, 49, 52
Palaces 16, 18
Persians 54, 61
Pharaohs 8, 14, 15, 16–17, 18, 22, 26, 27, 40–41, 43, 54, 55, 57, 61, 62
Poetry 39
Police 15

Pottery **8**, 8, 9, 11, 45
Priests and priestesses 15, 16, 19, **30**, 30, 31, 36, 43, 51, 54
Precious stones 7, 27
Ptolemies 54, 55, 56
Pyramids
 Egyptian 5, 6, 7, 11, 16, **41**, 40–41, 56, 58, 60, 61
 Mexican 5

Religion 11, 12, 13, 16, 28–37, 54, 61
Rome 54, 55, 56, 57, 61

Scarabs **29**, 28–29
Schools 18, 29
Scribes 15, **18**, 18, 19, 43, **51**, 51, 59
Sculptures 18, 29, 55, 55, 56
Servants 36, 38, 43, 51
Slavery 11, 14, 15, **24**, **25**, 24–25, 27, 36, 40, 50, 52
Soldiers **26**, 26

Temples 5, 11, 13, 14, 15, 16, 18, 19, 28, 30, 31, 38, **41**, 40–41, 51, 56, 59, 62
Tombs 5, 13, 15 16, 17, 18, 20, 22, 26, 27, 29, 33, 35, 36, 38, 40–41, 42, 43, 45, 48, 49, 50, 52, 58, 59, 60, 61
Tools 8, 9, 15, 22, 36, 47, 61
Towns 11, 21
Trade 6, 21, 25, 26, 27, 43, 55, 56
Transportation **6**, 6, 7
Tutankhamun **17**, 17, 20

Wars 26, 27, 55, 62
Women 14, 17, 31, 38, 43, 46, 50, 51, 52, 53, 60
Writing 9, 10, 18–19, 36, 38, 39.